Please visit our website, www.enslow.com.
For a free color catalog of all our high-quality books, call toll free
1-800-398-2504 or fax 1-877-980-4454.

Cataloging-in-Publication Data
Names: Emminizer, Theresa.
Title: Who cleans up oil spills? / Theresa Emminizer.
Description: Buffalo, NY : Enslow Publishing, 2025. | Series: Calling all community heroes! | Includes glossary and index.
Identifiers: ISBN 9781978542150 (pbk.) | ISBN 9781978542167 (library bound) | ISBN 9781978542174 (ebook)
Subjects: LCSH: Oil spills–Cleanup–Juvenile literature. | Oil spills–Environmental aspects–Juvenile literature. |
First responders–Juvenile literature.
Classification: LCC TD196.P4 E495 2025 | DDC 363.738'2–dc23

Published in 2025 by
Enslow Publishing
2544 Clinton Street
Buffalo, NY 14224

Copyright © 2025 Enslow Publishing

Designer: Tanya Dellaccio Keeney
Editor: Theresa Emminizer

Photo credits: Cover (background) ASTA DESIGN/Shutterstock.com; cover (speech bubble) mejorana/Shutterstock.com; cover (person) Aleksandar Malivuk/Shutterstock.com; cover (oil spill), pp. 5, 13 GreenOak/Shutterstock.com; p. 7 Eric Glenn/Shutterstock.com; p. 9 Mark Zannoni/Shutterstock.com; p. 11 PeopleImages.com - Yuri A/Shutterstock.com; p. 15 KARNT THASSANAPHAK/Shutterstock.com; p. 17 Corepics VOF/Shutterstock.com; p. 19 Tigergallery/Shutterstock.com; p. 21 MPH Photos/Shutterstock.com.

CPSIA compliance information: Batch #CWENS25: For further information contact Enslow Publishing, at 1-800-398-2504.

Find us on

CONTENTS

BOLDFACE WORDS APPEAR IN WORDS TO KNOW.

OH NO, OIL!

Oil is an important **resource** that's used for many purposes. But oil spills are very harmful! Who cleans up oil spills? Community heroes do! These heroes come in many forms, but they all work together to keep people and animals safe from oil spills.

OIL FLOATING ON THE SURFACE, OR TOP, OF THE WATER IS CALLED A SLICK.

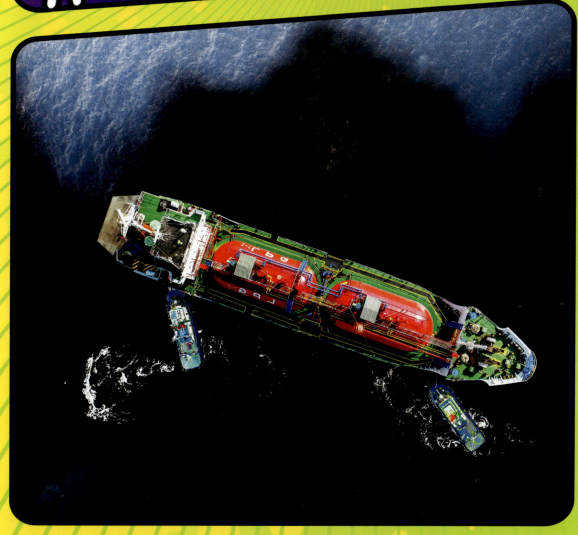

CALL THE COAST GUARD

First responders are people trained to help in **emergencies**. When oil spills in coastal and deepwater **ports**, the U.S. Coast Guard leads the **response**. The coast guard is a branch of the military, or armed forces. Its purpose is to keep American waters safe.

 MEMBERS OF THE COAST GUARD ARE CALLED COASTGUARDSMEN.

ALERT THE EPA

The Environmental Protection Agency (EPA) usually leads the response to oil spills in inland waters. These include any waters not part of the ocean, such as rivers or lakes. As its name suggests, the EPA keeps the environment, or natural world, safe. The EPA also works to keep people healthy and safe.

THE EPA HAS MANY SHIPS LIKE THE ONE PICTURED HERE.

U.S. ENVIRONMENTAL PROTECTION AGENCY

AID FROM THE NOAA

Scientists from the National Oceanic and **Atmospheric** Administration (NOAA) also help clean up oil spills. They may work closely with the coast guard or EPA to decide the best way to handle cleanup. They work to reduce, or lessen, the harm to people, animals, and the environment.

 A SCIENTIST IS SOMEONE WHO STUDIES, OR LEARNS ABOUT, THE WORLD AND HOW IT WORKS.

WHERE DOES OIL COME FROM?

Oil is a **liquid** that forms from plant and animal remains. It's found under the ground and the ocean floor. People drill for oil, pump it out, and transport, or move, it to plants called refineries. At a refinery, the oil is made into other things, such as gas.

THIS IS A TANKER, OR A LARGE SHIP WITH TANKS FOR CARRYING LIQUIDS SUCH AS OIL.

WHY DOES OIL SPILL?

There are many times during oil **extraction** or use that it may spill. Oil spills may happen during drilling. They often happen during transportation. Oil pipelines can burst, or break. Oil tankers may **leak** or even sink.

 EVEN SMALL OIL SPILLS CAN CAUSE GREAT HARM TO ANIMALS AND THEIR ENVIRONMENT.

WHAT'S THE HARM?

Oil spreads quickly in water. It kills and harms plants and animals. Some environments are unable to recover, or heal. It is toxic, or deadly, to people as well. People can have big health problems long after a spill has taken place.

 COMMUNITY HEROES HELP ANIMALS AFTER OIL SPILLS, SUCH AS BY CLEANING BIRDS' FEATHERS.

CLEANING UP SPILLS

First responders use floating tools called booms to block oil spills and move oil away from places where it's most harmful. Team members on boats use skimmers to skim, or remove, oil on the water's surface. Sometimes oil is burned away and broken up with **chemicals**.

FIRST RESPONDERS MUST WEAR PROTECTIVE GEAR, OR CLOTHING, TO KEEP THEMSELVES SAFE FROM OIL TOXINS.

HOW CAN WE HELP?

Every year, thousands of oil spills happen in U.S. waters. The coast guard, EPA, and NOAA work together to clean up oil spills and stop them from spreading. You can do your part too! Cut down on oil use by biking, walking, or carpooling.

SMALL CHANGES CAN MAKE A BIG DIFFERENCE! YOU CAN BE A COMMUNITY HERO TOO.

WORDS TO KNOW

atmospheric: Having to do with the atmosphere, or the mixture of gases that surround a planet.

chemical: Matter that can be mixed with other matter to cause changes.

emergency: An unexpected situation that needs quick action.

extraction: Obtaining a substance, such as oil or gas, from something or somewhere, often using machines.

leak: To let water or other liquids out.

liquid: Something that flows and takes the shape of the container holding it.

port: A place where ships may stay safe from storms.

resource: A usable supply of something.

response: Something that is a reaction to something else.

FOR MORE INFORMATION

BOOKS

Dicker, Katie. *Clean and Safe Water.* New York, NY: PowerKids Press, 2023.

West, Oliver and David West. *What on Earth Is Threatening Our Wildlife?* Buffalo, NY: Enslow Publishing, 2024.

WEBSITES

Environmental Protection Agency
epa.gov/oil-spills-prevention-and-preparedness-regulations
Find out more about how the EPA prevents and prepares for oil spills.

National Ocean Service
oceanservice.noaa.gov/education/tutorial-coastal/oil-spills/os03.html
Read this helpful page about what happens during and after an oil spill.

INDEX